THE CLANSMEN

THE CLANSMEN

R. D. LOBBAN

Illustrated by Gareth Floyd

 University of London Press Ltd

Contents

I · *The Highland Clans*

THE year was 1750, and the little café in Paris was crowded. At one table sat a tall, splendidly-built man in Highland dress. Nearby there was a group of seven Frenchmen, and from time to time they would make joking comments about his appearance. The Highlander, Donald MacDonald, tried to ignore them, but the Frenchmen grew steadily bolder and more insulting.

"Know you that Paris is full of these Highland savages," declared one in a loud voice.

"And their leader, the so-called Prince Charles, is also come here," laughed another. "Paris could well do without such a fool and his half-clad followers. The English were wise to chase them all out of their country."

This was too much for the Highlander. In one swift action he rose from the table, drew out his dirk (or dagger), and strode over towards his tormentors. His face a blaze of anger, he halted beside the seven Frenchmen. His eyes swept over each man in turn, and then he threw the dirk down on the table in front of them.

"Insolent dogs!" he thundered. "You have insulted my Prince and my people. For that you must give me your apologies or we shall settle the matter with our swords."

"You are bold, Highlander," sneered one of the Frenchmen. "But since you have challenged us, you shall have satisfaction. Choose one of us to fight. Take Pierre here. He is the poorest swordsman," he added with a laugh.

"Not one, monsieur," the Highlander said softly. "I shall fight

you all—that is if you are not just cowards and boasters. There is an open space behind the inn. The innkeeper will be my second."

Their mirth and jollity quite vanished, the Frenchmen followed the innkeeper and the Highlander outside. And very quickly they discovered that their opponent was a master swordsman. One after the other they faced him, but none could match his deadly skill. Soon it was all over. Three of the Frenchmen lay dead, and the other four were seriously injured. The insult to the Highlander's people had been wiped out in blood.

THE HIGHLANDS   Donald MacDonald had fought for Prince Charles in the Jacobite Rebellion of 1745 (see p. 48) and had been forced to flee to France. His home was in the Highlands of Scotland, that part of the country lying north and west of a line running from Stonehaven in the north-east to Helensburgh on the Clyde (see map opposite p. 10). It is a mountainous area with great ranges of hills, broken by steep-sided valleys. In the west, sea lochs penetrate deep into the heart of the country, while off the west coast lie the islands of the Hebrides.

THE HIGHLAND CLANS For many centuries before 1750 the Highlands had been the homeland of numerous clans. A clan was a community of people who claimed they were descended from a common ancestor. The word "clan" (or "clann") originally meant children, and the clansmen were regarded as the children of the founder of the clan. The founder might have been called Donald, and so the members of the clan were called MacDonald or son of Donald, "mac" being the Gaelic word for son. In earlier times, however, ordinary people in the Highlands did not normally use surnames. A man might be a member of the Clan MacDonald, but he would be known by such a title as Colin, son of Duncan, and not Colin MacDonald. In the Highlands today, many people still speak of their neighbours in this way instead of using their surnames.

The first clans were probably formed in the thirteenth century. Initially a clan might be confined to one particular glen or valley, but as time went on it might extend its territories until it controlled large areas. As a clan grew larger, important branches or "septs" would appear. These septs sometimes adopted different names, but they were still a real part of the clan.

THE CHIEF A clan was ruled by a chief, who was immensely powerful. He was regarded as the head of the family and as the direct descendant of the founder of the clan. Normally he would be succeeded by his eldest son, but the new chief would have to show that he was fit to lead the clan. If he did not prove himself brave and courageous in battle, then the clan might select another member of the old chief's family to rule them. But once a chief was accepted, then the clansmen would be utterly loyal to him, and at all times they would be ready and willing to sacrifice their lives for him.

The devotion of the clansmen to their chiefs is well illustrated by the famous story of an old Highlander named MacLean and his seven sons. The MacLeans were part of a Scottish army fighting against Oliver Cromwell at Inverkeithing in 1651, and during the battle they and their chief, Sir Hector MacLean, were surrounded by the English. At once the old man and his sons formed a circle round the chief. When a blow was aimed at him, one of them would thrust himself in front of the chief, crying out: "Another for Hector". Soon all eight lay dead, and only then could the enemy strike down the chief. In memory of their bravery, the Clan MacLean adopted the words "Another for Hector" as their war-cry.

LAW AND ORDER   One of the main tasks of the chiefs was to maintain law and order in their territories. They held courts and inflicted punishments on any clansmen who broke their laws. For serious offences they would even impose the death sentence.

MACPHERSON   Most of the clansmen were prepared to obey the laws and customs of their clans, but a few rebelled and left their homes to live as outlaws. One of the most notorious of all the Highland outlaws was James Macpherson from Banffshire who lived in the seventeenth century. Like Robin Hood, he was beloved of the ordinary people, for he often took money and

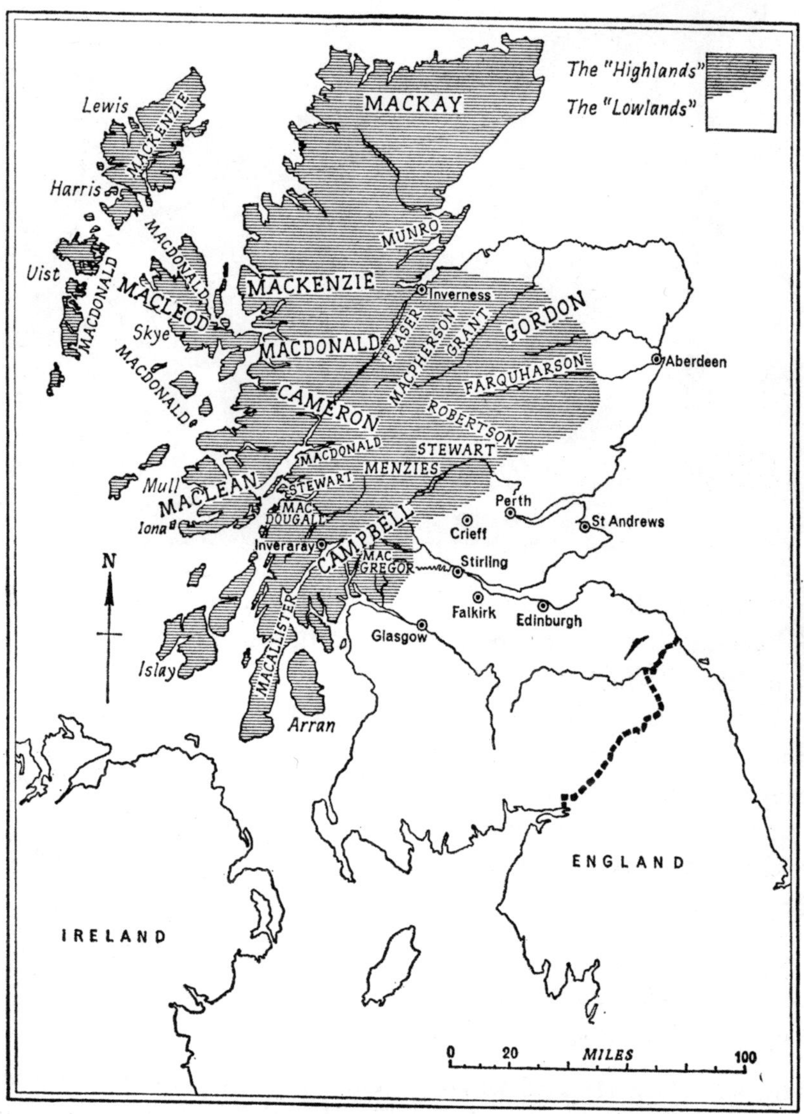

Some clan territories in Scotland, in the early seventeenth century

goods from the wealthy to give to the poor. He was also a fine
fiddler and would often play a merry tune when preparing to rob
some travellers.

But at last James Macpherson was captured by the authorities
and sentenced to death. When he was led to the gallows, he
played a tune called "Macpherson's Lament", which had been
specially composed for his execution. The memory of his courage
and merry spirits has lived on, and the song is still a favourite in
Scotland:

> Sae rantinly, sae wantonly, sae dauntinly gaed he.
> He played a tune and danced it roon'
> Below the gallows tree.

THE CLANS AND THE KING   Cut off as they were from the
rest of Scotland by mountain barriers, the Highland clans were for

many centuries practically independent. The kings of Scotland did try to bring their Highland subjects under control, but as it was difficult to lead large armies through the Highlands, rulers were sometimes forced to take desperate measures. James I, for instance, invited some rebellious Highland chiefs to a great banquet at Inverness in 1428. When each chief arrived, he was seized and thrown into a dungeon.

A few years later, King James was himself slain by some of his subjects. Other kings were equally unsuccessful in bringing the Highlands permanently under their rule; and it was only in the eighteenth century that they were finally brought completely under Government control.

THE MACDONALDS   One of the most powerful of all the clans in the early centuries were the MacDonalds. They were descended from a twelfth-century chieftain named Somerled who had driven the Norsemen out of southern Argyll. Somerled's son, Dugall, founded the Clan MacDougall, while his grandson, Donald, was the founder of Clan Donald or the MacDonalds. A later MacDonald chief, Angus Og (Young Angus), fought with Robert the Bruce against the English at Bannockburn in 1314.

Over the years the power of the MacDonald chiefs steadily increased. In 1346 they began to call themselves Lords of the Isles, and they ruled like princes over a huge territory stretching from Kintyre in the south to Ross in the north. There were various branches of the clan: the Clanranald, Keppoch, Sleat and MacIan branches; and together they made up the dominant force in the Highlands.

The position of the MacDonalds, however, alarmed the Scottish kings, and they struggled to weaken them. In 1494 James IV took over the title of the Lord of the Isles, and since that time the heir to the throne has always held the title. (Prince Charles is the present Lord of the Isles.) Later, when the MacDonalds rebelled, some of their lands were taken from them. Other clans who had been jealous of the MacDonalds also seized their lands, and by the beginning of the seventeenth century they had lost much of their former power and glory.

THE CAMPBELLS   The decline of the MacDonalds was accompanied by the growth of rival clans such as the Campbells. The name is "cam beul" in Gaelic, meaning wry or crooked mouth, and was probably first used to describe an early Campbell chief. By the early seventeenth century the Campbells controlled much of Argyllshire and Perthshire. Their leaders were given various titles by the Scottish kings until in 1701 one of the chiefs was created Duke of Argyll. As they grew more powerful, the Campbells now became the clan which most aroused the fears and jealousies of their rivals, and they were disliked and hated by many other clans.

One of the early leaders of the Campbells was known as "Cailean Mor" or "Big Colin", and since then the chief has been called "Mac Cailein Mor" or the son of Big Colin. The Campbells were very proud of their chiefs and believed they were the equal of any king. In the nineteenth century, when Queen Victoria's daughter Louise was being married to the eldest son of the Duke of Argyll, some Campbells felt that it was the young princess who was making a good match. "Isn't it proud the Queen will be this day that her daughter has got the son of Mac Cailein Mor for her husband," they declared boastfully.

OTHER CLANS   While the Campbells were becoming power-ful in the south-west Highlands, another clan, the MacKenzies, came to be dominant in the north. Their chiefs became the Earls of Seaforth, and they controlled the island of Lewis and much of Inverness, Ross and Sutherland. Another powerful clan was the Gordons under their chief, the Earl of Huntly, who held lands in Aberdeen, Banff and Lochaber. Other prominent clans were the Camerons in Lochaber, the Stewarts in Appin and Perthshire, Clan Chattan in Inverness, the MacLeods in Skye, the MacDougalls in Lorn, and the MacLeans in Mull. (See map opposite p. 10 for other clans.)

For many centuries the various clans continued to live and flourish in the Highlands of Scotland. In this book we shall study their lives and customs as they existed in the seventeenth century, as well as interesting events of earlier and later times. Over the years, however, the clansmen's way of life did not change very much, and thus the description given could quite easily refer to the lives lived by many Highlanders throughout the period from the thirteenth to the eighteenth centuries.

2 · *Life in the Glens*

CASTLES   The Highlands of Scotland form a very hilly and mountainous region, and there have never been many towns or even large villages compared with the Lowlands. The main centres in the various clan areas were the chiefs' mansions or castles. These were often situated on a rock or small peninsula to make them more easily defended. They were normally several storeys high, the kitchens being on the ground floor, the great hall on the first floor, and the apartments of the chief and his family on the upper floors.

Frequently the castle was surrounded by a wall, and in the courtyard there were several small buildings which were used as stables and sleeping quarters for the chief's servants and body-guard. There were also pipers, a bard (or poet), and perhaps a harpist living at the castle. These were very important figures in the clan, and many of the bards and harpists had studied literature and music in Ireland. The bard wrote poems and songs telling of

the glorious events in the clan's history. In battle he would fight close to the chief so that later he could write of his courage and brave deeds.

The office of clan piper was a particularly coveted one, and sometimes certain families in the clan would become hereditary pipers. The MacCrimmons were the hereditary pipers of the Clan MacLeod, for instance, and in the sixteenth century they helped to found a College of Piping in Skye.

One of the duties of the clan pipers was to play during meals in the great hall of the castle. The chief and his family ate at a raised table at one end of the hall, and his bard, harpist, servants and bodyguard ate at lower tables. On special occasions ordinary clansfolk might be invited to the castle. A huge fire would blaze on stone slabs in the middle of the floor, and there would be great feasting and merry-making. After the meal, the harpist would play his harp or clarsach, the piper his bagpipes, and the bard would recite favourite poems and stories. There might also be dancing, wrestling and games and amusements.

CLAN LANDS   All the clan lands belonged to the chief, and an extensive area round the castle was kept for his own use. The rest of the land was let out in large estates to near relatives or kinsmen of the chief known as cadets. These cadets lived in small two-roomed stone farmhouses, and they paid a rent to the chief for their land. In time of war the cadets became the officers of the clan forces.

CLACHAN   The cadets retained part of their estates in their own hands, and then they sub-let the remainder to the ordinary clansmen. In return for their land, the clansmen worked on the estates of the cadets and the chief, and also handed over some of their produce and their livestock. Normally a certain area of land would be given to a group of clansmen who lived together in clachans – small settlements of four, eight or perhaps twelve houses. Often a clachan would be situated by the side of a stream running through a glen or close to the shores of a loch.

The houses in a clachan were usually small rectangular buildings with two rooms. The larger one was for the family and the smaller one housed cows, goats and hens. The walls were from three to six feet thick and were constructed of rubble-stone or turf. The roof was made of turf, and then covered with thatch or heather.

Inside, the houses were dark and gloomy, for there were no windows. Sometimes the Highlanders used a lamp burning seal oil, but normally the only light came from the peat fire that burnt night and day in the middle of the earthen floor. Over it was hung a large iron cooking pot. There was no chimney, and smoke escaped through a small hole in the roof. The only furniture was a few stools, a wooden bench and a chest. There might also be

Eilean Donan Castle

a rough wooden box bed filled with heather; but many clansmen were quite happy to sleep on a pile of heather laid on the floor. This all might seem very primitive, but it should perhaps be remembered that many people in all the countries of Europe in the seventeenth century were living in rather similar conditions.

DRESS   Although the houses of the ordinary clansmen were not so very different from those in other countries, their dress was peculiarly their own. The men did not wear breeches, and since they left a large part of their thighs bare, they were known as "Red Shanks". Some went barefoot, but most wore shoes made of hide or deerskin and long woollen stockings tied under the knees with pieces of straw. They had dark yellow shirts which reached half-way down their thighs; above this a short tunic or jacket and a long rectangular piece of woollen cloth called a plaid; and on their heads a large blue bonnet. The plaid was wrapped round the waist, pulled into pleats with a belt, and the end of it was thrown over the shoulder and fastened firmly to the clansman's breast with a pin. Later, in the eighteenth century, this developed into the kilt, which was in effect the lower half of the plaid with the pleats stitched up.

The clothes worn by the ordinary clansmen were all rough home-made garments, but the stockings and plaids were dyed in attractive colours. Dyes were obtained from the lichen and other plants, and Highland women were skilled in weaving tartans with intricate patterns. There were no special clan patterns or tartans as there are today, but many clansmen wore emblems such as sprigs of heather to indicate their clan.

WOMEN   The wives and mothers of the clansmen wore long-sleeved, ankle-length woollen or linen dresses, and in cold weather they draped woollen plaids round their shoulders. Normally the plaid was white with a few stripes of red, black or blue. They also wore woollen socks or stockings, and shoes of hide or deerskin. Young women went bare-headed, but after they were married they wore a mutch—a head-dress made of linen that was tied under the chin. Young and old liked to make themselves pretty, and they had several beauty preparations to improve their complexions. Mothers advised their daughters to wash their faces "with a lotion of goat's milk and sweet violets", and promised them that if they did then "there's not a king's son but will run after thee".

THE CHIEF'S COSTUME   The clothes of the chiefs and their families were much finer than those of the ordinary clansfolk. A chief's plaid was made of the very best wool, and his shirt had lace at the collar and sleeves. Chiefs often wore trews, a kind of tartan trousers, for these were more convenient for horse riding.

18th-century clan chief, his lady and a clansman

In the eighteenth century the chiefs began to wear kilts with coloured stockings. The chief's wife and daughters wore beautiful, full-length silk or linen dresses, and these they adorned with jewels and precious stones. Out of doors they wore a plaid fastened at the breast with silver buckles.

CRAFTSMEN   Sometimes the chiefs purchased their fine clothes in the Lowlands, but more often they were made by local tailors and shoemakers. While they were carrying out their work, the craftsmen would live in the castles or houses of the chiefs and the richer cadets. They were given food, lodgings and a small payment. Other craftsmen to be found in a clachan were carpenters, armourers and smiths. The blacksmiths in particular were highly skilled, and often produced very fine work in iron.

FARMING   Yet although there were several craftsmen in the Highland glens, the principal occupation of the clansmen was farming. Each clachan had its portion of land owned and worked jointly by the inhabitants. The arable was divided into the infield and outfield, the infield being the more fertile land near the clachan, and the outfield the rougher land further off. When the land was being ploughed, each man would bring a horse to help pull the heavy wooden ploughs; but if the land was hilly they would work together using wooden spades called caschroms.

When the land was ploughed, it was divided into strips. Each inhabitant was then given a certain number of strips scattered here and there throughout the infield and outfield. Sometimes the strips were allocated by lot so that each man would have his chance of obtaining the best land. The main crops grown were oats, barley, and perhaps some flax for making linen.

HERDS   Beyond the infield and outfield was the pasture land. Many areas of the Highlands were much more suited to rearing animals than growing crops, and each clachan would have large herds of cattle, sheep and goats. The cattle were a small black, red or brown breed that were the ancestors of the Highland cattle of today. There were also great herds on the estates of the chiefs and the cadets.

OTHER TASKS   In addition to looking after their herds and crops, the clansmen had many other tasks to perform. From time to time they re-thatched their houses, and repaired walls and dykes. In the summer they cut and stacked huge piles of peat to provide a plentiful supply of fuel for the fires during the winter. The womenfolk, too, had numerous tasks and duties. Not only did they cook, bake, spin, weave, make the family clothes, and undertake all the household chores, but they also looked after the hens, milked the cows, and helped in the fields at harvest time.

THE SHEILINGS   During the summer months, the womenfolk were particularly busy. The cattle were taken from the glens to pasturelands high in the hills known as shielings; and for many weeks the women and girls would spend much of their time making butter and cheese for the winter. While they were on the shielings, the clansfolk lived in rough huts of turf and sods, but everyone enjoyed their time there. The children roamed and played in the hills, and looked on it all as a glorious holiday.

DROVING   In the autumn the cattle were taken back to the clachan. Soon afterwards many of the animals were slaughtered and the meat salted, for the clansmen did not have sufficient winter feed to keep them alive till the spring. Large numbers of the cattle, however, were sold in the Lowlands. Men known as drovers would buy up cattle throughout a whole district, and when they had gathered a large herd, they began driving it south. The cattle were sold at markets at Crieff or Falkirk, and with the money they received the clansmen purchased grain, weapons, iron pots, and other goods they could not produce themselves.

TRANSPORT   Goods being taken from the Lowlands to the Highlands were carried by pack-horses. There were no proper roads in the Highlands, and thus there were few carts or coaches. Chiefs and the wealthier cadets rode on horseback, but the ordinary clansmen travelled on foot.

FOOD   The clansmen's herds of sheep and cattle provided them with a substantial diet of beef, mutton, butter, milk and cheese. They also ate porridge, oatcakes baked on a girdle hung over the fire, and vegetables like beans, peas and cabbages. The food was served in wooden bowls and eaten with knives or wooden spoons. In earlier times the clansmen's favourite drink was ale, but in later centuries many Highlanders came to prefer whisky, a drink which they themselves distilled. They claimed that they needed a strong drink to help them withstand the cold wet climate of their northern glens!

FISHING AND HUNTING   Those clansmen who lived near the coast or on the islands added to their food supplies by fishing, while those who lived inland might catch salmon in a nearby stream or river. The Highlanders also trapped and hunted wild fowls, grouse, geese and red deer. Sometimes the chiefs would organise a great expedition to hunt deer, and all the clansmen would take part.

FAMINE   After a successful hunt, the clansfolk would feast on rich venison for several weeks, but there were times when they were not so fortunate. In the spring, after they had eaten all the salted meat they had stored in the autumn, they could suffer severe hunger. At such times they would be forced to bleed their cattle and then mix the blood with oatmeal. In really difficult years they might even have to eat seaweed or a soup made from herbs and nettles.

HEALTH   Yet though the Highlanders at times suffered real hunger, they were in the main a healthy people. Their clachans and glens were not overcrowded, and they escaped many of the plagues and epidemics that struck down so many people living in towns. They lived an active outdoor life hunting and looking after their herds, and this made them hardy and fit.

SPORTS   Many of the games of the clansmen, too, helped to make them strong and healthy. They played shinty, and they often held contests in running, swimming, fencing ,wrestling and tossing

Tossing the caber

the caber or pine-trunk. Shinty resembles hockey, but the players use a longer, thinner stick and strike the leather or wooden ball with much more power and force than hockey players do. This game is still played by teams in northern Scotland.

CEILIDHS   During the long dark nights of winter, when they could not take part in sports, the Highlanders frequently held ceilidhs in each other's homes. All the inhabitants of a clachan would come along to the house of one clansman, and each person in turn would entertain the others. They might recite a poem, tell stories of ancient clan heroes, or sing a favourite song. The Highlanders were extremely fond of singing, and they had many working songs to sing when they were carrying out various tasks. They had songs for spinning and weaving, for churning, for reaping, and for rowing a boat. They had also a type of song called "puirt-a-beul" or mouth music, to which the people could dance when there were no musical instruments available.

MARRIAGES   In the same way that all the inhabitants of a clachan would attend the ceilidhs, so they would all join together to celebrate special occasions such as weddings. When a young couple were being married, everyone gave a present, everyone was invited, and all brought food and drink to the wedding feast. The festivities were held in the bride's house. There would be singing and dancing, and the merrymaking would continue long into the night until everyone was exhausted. But next day they would begin all over again, and so the celebrations might continue for several days.

In the Highlands it was customary for young people to make their own choice of a partner. But sometimes the chiefs would arrange marriages for lonely widows and widowers, and occasionally a man would ask a neighbour to find a partner for him. One clansman even sent a friend to buy a wife for him on the island of Lewis for a shilling!

FESTIVALS   The traditional festivals of the year, particularly New Year and Hallowe'en, were other occasions when the clansfolk liked to celebrate. At Hallowe'en

17th-century bagpipes

the children dressed up as goblins and went round all the houses in the clachan. Everyone gave them presents to seek the favour throughout the following year of those spirits the children represented.

CHILDREN   Though the children played a special part in the Hallowe'en festivities, their ordinary lives did not differ so very much from those of their parents. They wore similar clothes, and they were required to help and assist their fathers and mothers in all the work and duties of the family. Nevertheless, children in the Highland glens must have led adventurous lives. Besides joining in all the amusements of the adults, they could explore the hills and mountains, fish in streams or lochs and climb cliffs searching for eagles' eyries or nests. Like their parents, they grew to love their Highland hills and glens, and they had no desire to live elsewhere.

Clarsach

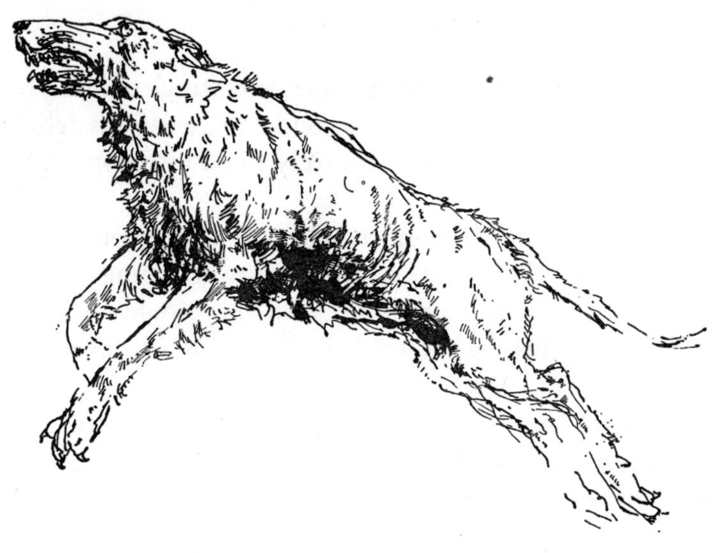

3 · *Raids and Feuds*

MUCH as the clansmen loved their homes and their Highland glens, they often grew restless. They were not particularly fond of farming, and believed that a man's real job was to hunt and to fight in battle. From an early age they were brought up to be bold and fearless, and to look forward to the day when they could fight against their people's enemies in battle.

The sons of chiefs were expected to be especially courageous, and sometimes they would be set a stern test to prove their superior prowess. Such a test was given to Ian MacKay, the son of a fifteenth-century chief. He was summoned into the dining-chamber of his father's castle, where he found the tables heaped with food; but in front of the tables stood a fierce and savage hound. As the boy entered, the hound snarled and leapt towards him. Quickly Ian pulled out his dirk and struck skilfully at its throat, killing the hound in a few seconds. The chief was delighted, for he now knew that his son was truly fitted to become a leader of his people.

Not only were the clansmen bold and courageous, but also extremely hardy. They were accustomed to tramping long miles in rough mountainous countryside, and they could sleep out of doors in all weathers. They used their plaid as a blanket, and in winter they would often dip it in a stream before wrapping it round them. The Highlanders were also rather scornful of weaklings, and one Cameron clansman was extremely angry with his son when on a campaign he made a large snowball for a pillow. "Are you become like a woman that you cannot sleep without such luxury?" he demanded contemptuously.

CLAN FORCES   Since they were such a brave and hardy people, the clansmen made excellent warriors. In the early eighteenth century, the Campbells could raise about 5,000 fighting men and the MacKenzies about 2,500, and they were therefore powerful military forces. Other clans, however, were much smaller. The Camerons, for instance, had 800 men, the MacLeans 500, and the MacDonalds of Glencoe only about 130 men.

THE FIERY CROSS   All the clans, whether large or small, were frequently involved in war and skirmishes. The clansmen were summoned to a campaign by means of a fiery cross that was sent round the clan territories. This consisted of two pieces of wood made into the form of a cross. From one end of the cross hung a piece of cloth stained with blood, while the other end was set alight. Several runners would carry a cross in different directions,

and when it was sighted each clansman would at once stop whatever he was doing. Swiftly he would seize his weapons and set off for the mustering point of the clan. Most clansmen would have a claymore or big sword, a dirk, and a round shield. The shield was made of wood and covered with hide, and in the centre there was a small spike or boss. Some clansmen carried axes, and in later times a few would have muskets.

CATTLE RAIDS   Many of the expeditions undertaken by the clansmen were raids against other clans to seize their herds of sheep and cattle. The Highlanders did not regard this practice as stealing. They declared that since God had created all animals and these fed on God's pastures, they belonged to all men!

Sometimes the whole fighting force of a clan would take part in a cattle raid, but normally the raids were carried out by small parties of young men. Led perhaps by the chief's son, they marched by hill paths towards the territory of a rival clan. When they approached their goal, they waited till after nightfall. Then silently they swooped down on the herds. The guards protecting

the animals were swiftly overpowered, and the raiders hurriedly drove the herds back towards their own glens.

Speed was vital, for the owners of the herds always gave chase. Sometimes they managed to overtake the raiders, and there followed a short, fierce clash. But more often the raiders were too swift for the pursuers, and returned to their glens in triumph with their booty. When this happened there would be great rejoicing, and some of the stolen animals would be slaughtered to provide meat for a great celebration feast.

RAIDS ON THE LOWLANDS   The Highlanders also made frequent raids on the herds in the Lowlands. The people there could do little to stop them, for they knew all the paths through the hills. So the authorities attempted to enlist the support of friendly clans to form a defence force under an official called a Constable.

ROB ROY MACGREGOR   One of the most famous of these Constables was Rob Roy MacGregor. He was born in 1671 at Balquhidder in Perthshire, and was a member of a clan long noted for its lawless deeds. In 1603 the clan had been outlawed by the Scottish king, and the clansmen were forbidden to use the name MacGregor on pain of death.

In his early days Rob Roy had been a most successful cattle raider, but the authorities hoped that since he knew all the tricks and tactics of the Highlanders, he would be able to stop their attacks. But Rob Roy did not always act as they had hoped. Even as Constable he continued to engage in raiding, and he also demanded money from Lowland farmers to pay for his protection from other clansmen.

Rob Roy had a most adventurous career. He fought for the Jacobites in the 1715 Rebellion, and he took part in many duels. On several occasions he was captured by the authorities, but each time he escaped. He died in 1734 after being wounded in a duel, and he was buried in the churchyard at Balquhidder where his grave can still be seen. Later Sir Walter Scott wrote a novel about his exploits, but he depicted Rob Roy as a romantic hero instead of the brave scoundrel that he actually was.

CLAN FEUDS   Over the years many fierce feuds had sprung up between rival clans, and these led to bitter and deadly battles. For long the MacDonalds feuded with the Campbells, and countless other clans were pitted against each other.

Clan feuds were started in many different ways. Sometimes they arose out of a cattle raid; sometimes the members of one clan would insult the men of another; and sometimes there would be bitter feelings when a marriage arranged between a man and woman of two clans broke down. This last cause brought about a quarrel between the Campbells and the MacLeans in the sixteenth century. Lachlan MacLean, a leading member of Clan

MacLean, had married a relative of the Earl of Argyll, but after a time he grew tired of his wife. He ordered some of his men to seize her and to place her on a rock lying between the islands of Lismore and Mull. Fortunately a boat happened to pass by, and she was rescued. Her relatives swore vengeance, and shortly afterwards Lachlan MacLean was killed by her brother.

Sometimes in their feuds the clansmen could be very cruel, but much more frequently they acted nobly towards their enemies. After a battle, they would normally allow their defeated enemies to go free, and those who had fought bravely against them would be praised and honoured.

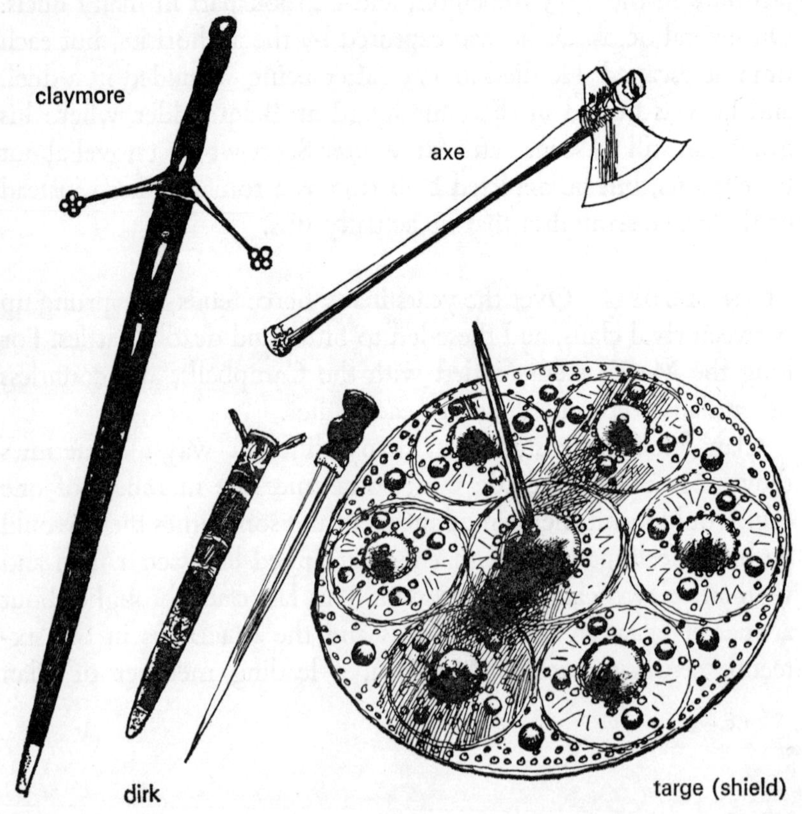

4 · *Spirit and Culture of the Clans*

HIGHLAND HOSPITALITY   Although for several centuries there were many bitter feuds in the Highlands, we must not exaggerate the amount of fighting that went on. Most clans lived on very good terms with their neighbours, and there were frequent inter-marriages. The clansfolk were also very hospitable, and they were always ready to give a welcome to men from other clans who passed through their territories. Their custom was that once a guest had been entertained in a Highland home, then he could not be attacked, even if it were later discovered that he was an enemy of the clan. In the same way, the guest was under an obligation to refrain from doing any injury to his host.

A noted example of these laws of Highland hospitality occurred during a quarrel between a certain William Munro and a member of the MacLeod clan who had written a poem insulting the Munros. William Munro swore that he would kill the poet, but failed to recognise him when he stopped at an inn where Munro was dining. And when MacLeod offered him a drink, he readily accepted. Later he asked the stranger his name, and he gave a shout of anger on learning it was his sworn enemy. But he had drunk with MacLeod, and so now he could not kill him. Instead of fighting the two men began to talk, and in a short time they became good friends.

MASSACRE OF GLENCOE   In contrast with the conduct of William Munro was the action of a party of Government troops in 1692. MacIan, chief of the MacDonalds of Glencoe, had been late in taking the oath of loyalty to the new King, William of

Orange, and the Government decided to punish him severely. A party of troops under the command of Colin Campbell of Glenlyon was billeted on the MacDonalds. Then after living with their hosts for a fortnight, they set about massacring them at dead of night. The chief was murdered, his wife was driven out naked to die in the snow, and many of the clansfolk were butchered. All Highlanders were horrified at this breach of the laws of hospitality, and the whole affair showed that the Governments in Edinburgh and in London were in some ways less civilised than the Highlanders.

EDUCATION   In other ways, too, the Highlanders showed that their standards of civilisation were just as high as those in other parts of the country. Many of the chiefs and cadets were highly educated men, for it was customary for the clan leaders to send their sons to the universities of St Andrews, Glasgow, Aberdeen or Edinburgh, or even to Oxford, Cambridge, Paris or Holland. Their ladies were also well educated, for though they did not attend university they were often taught at home by tutors.

Just how educated and learned a clan leader might be is well illustrated by the story of one chieftain who was forced to go into exile in Rome after the Rebellion of 1745 (see p. 48). There he was visited by a cardinal who had heard of the chief's reputation for learning. To test him, the cardinal addressed him in seven different languages: in Latin, French, Italian, German, Spanish, Greek and English. Each time the chief replied without hesitation in the appropriate language. Then as the cardinal was leaving, the chief spoke to his Highland attendants in Gaelic asking them to show him out. The cardinal was quite crestfallen, for whereas the chief had known all the languages he himself could speak, he knew at least one of which the cardinal was quite ignorant.

GAELIC LITERATURE   Gaelic, of course, was the language spoken by all Highlanders in the seventeenth century. It is a Celtic language, just as are Irish Gaelic, Welsh, Manx, Breton and Cornish. Lowlanders and Englishmen felt that Gaelic was a barbaric tongue, but in fact many fine poems and works of literature have been written in it. In the seventeenth century there were a number of gifted poets, among them John MacDonald of Lochaber, who wrote several beautiful poems which are still read and studied today.

ORDINARY CLANSMEN   Yet though some of the Highland chiefs were highly educated men who could speak Gaelic and

Spinning, weaving and carding wool

many other languages, few of the ordinary clansmen received any formal education whatsoever. There were a few schools in the Highlands, but most children lived too far away from one to be able to attend. Instead they received a practical training from their parents in all the many skills necessary for their lives in the Highland glens. Boys were taught how to farm, how to fish and handle boats, how to hunt, and how to use weapons; girls were instructed in weaving, in the dyeing of clothes, and in a host of other tasks. In addition the Highland children also received a valuable form of education in the customs and culture of their people. They learnt the history and legends of the Highlands, they were taught to sing and to love music, and to respect and honour the bards.

LEGENDS   Many of the stories and legends that were told over and over again by the bards and at ceilidhs were based on certain ancient poems and myths. Some of these told of a group of legendary heroes named the Feinn, who had lived in the early centuries A.D., and who had performed great and heroic deeds. Many Highlanders believed that the Feinn had lived in Glencoe and that they had sailed out on their galleys to glorious adventures in the Hebrides and in Ireland.

FIONN   The King of Feinn was a brave leader called Fionn. One of the favourite stories about him told how on one occasion he was captured by the Norsemen. The Norsemen decided to kill him and left him alone and unarmed in the Great Glen near Loch Ness, where roamed a fierce, mad dog known as Grey Dog. When the Grey Dog scented Fionn, he came snarling and howling down the glen. But just as he was about to leap for Fionn's throat, he caught sight of the gold dog's collar round his arm. This belonged to Fionn's favourite hound, Bran, and at the sight of it Grey Dog became suddenly calm and gentle. Instead of savaging Fionn to death, he began to lick his legs. For a moment Fionn was puzzled, but then he understood. Grey Dog was the long lost brother of Bran, and he had recognised the collar and Bran's master. Swiftly Fionn and Grey Dog left the glen before the Norsemen could discover that their victim had not been killed.

DEIRDRE   One of the most tragic figures of these early stories and legends was Deirdre, the daughter of Column the Harper in Ireland. Connacher, King of Ulster, wished to marry her, but Deirdre loved a youth named Naoise, and she fled with him to Scotland. They lived in Glen Etive for many years, and Deirdre was very, very happy there. But one day a messenger arrived from Ireland and told them that King Connacher had forgiven them and wished them to return. Naoise was eager to go, and though Deirdre pleaded with him to stay in Scotland, they eventually set sail for Ireland. But no sooner had they landed than Naoise was killed by King Connacher's men and Deirdre was captured. She was now told that she must marry Connacher, but she was determined to remain faithful to her dead husband. One day, as she was being driven forth in a chariot, she suddenly rose up and leapt wildly to the ground. As she fell, her head struck a stone and she died. Many songs and poems have been written about this beautiful girl and her tragic fate.

TIR-NAN-OG   Another famous hero of the olden days was Ossian, the poet and bard of the Feinn. Ossian had an only son named Oscar, and when the lad died, Ossian grew sad and weary of life. One day, as he was walking by the shore, a fair maiden called Niamh, the daughter of the King of Youth, appeared before him. She invited him to follow her, and they sailed westward across the sea to the Islands of the Blest, or Tir-nan-Og, the land of eternal youth. Tir-nan-Og became a beautiful dream for many Highlanders, and they loved to speak of that wonderful place away out over the seas beyond the Hebrides where they would remain young for ever.

RELIGION   The stories about Fionn, Deirdre and Ossian all referred to a period before Christianity had been brought to the Highlands, but Highland boys and girls would also hear many tales about the early Christian saints and missionaries who had come to Scotland. The most famous of these was St Columba, who had come from Ireland to the island of Iona in 563 A.D. In the years that followed he had many adventures travelling through the Highlands and converting the kings and peoples of the area. Later the Highlands were brought under the control of the Roman

Iona Cathedral today

Church, and priests were settled in Highland parishes as they were in other parts of Scotland.

Up until the sixteenth century, Scotland, including the Highlands, was a Roman Catholic country, but in 1560 the Scottish Parliament broke the ties with the Pope in Rome. The Lowlands became overwhelmingly Protestant, and a Protestant Church was established. Many of the Highland chiefs and clans also accepted the new form of religion, but several of the clans and some of the islands like Barra and South Uist remained devoutly Catholic. Later in the eighteenth and nineteenth centuries, an extreme form of Protestantism gained support in several areas in the Highlands and Islands. This led to many of the Highland people becoming very strict in their observance of the Sabbath. Today tourists discover that they cannot travel by boat on a Sunday, and even find it very difficult to obtain accommodation on that day.

SUPERSTITIONS   Though Christianity came at an early date to the Highlands, the people there nevertheless continued to believe

41

in many strange superstitions. They were convinced, for instance, that there were spirits and fairies all around them, and they were quite certain that the fairies were continually playing tricks on human beings. Sometimes the fairies tempted people into their dwellings below the ground, where they were entertained so well with music and dancing that they did not realise how swiftly the hours, days and weeks were passing.

At other times fairies could be more spiteful. Sometimes they shot arrows at the clansmen's animals, and soon they would begin to waste away with sickness. Worst of all was the habit the fairies had of exchanging their children for human infants. The Highlanders tried to prevent them from approaching their babies by placing a piece of iron near the cot, but sometimes the fairies were still able to make the exchange. Thus if an infant appeared sickly or did not resemble its parents, the clansfolk would begin to fear that the worst had happened. Then they might decide to drop the child in a river, expose it for a night on a hill, or hold it over a fire to see if it were indeed a fairy. Here the belief in fairies could have quite terrible consequences.

Highlanders also believed that there were certain human beings who had special powers such as the gift of "second sight". This enabled them to "see" events that were happening in distant places, or events that had happened in the past or would occur in the future. The men and women who possessed this power were regarded with awe and some dread by their neighbours.

Other individuals who aroused the dread of the clansmen were those who had the power of the "evil eye". This meant that they could cause disaster and misfortune merely by glancing angrily at their neighbours or their neighbours' livestock. Even more feared were those women who had made a bargain with the Devil and had become witches. Witches had the power to raise storms and sink ships, they could strike down a man's cattle and children with fatal diseases, and could change themselves into cats and hares.

CURES   In their treatment of illness, too, the clansmen were often very superstitious. They had many weird cures, and relied on several charms and spells. Sore eyes, for instance, could be cured if the patient spat in a vessel of clear water and chanted this verse:

A charm for sore smarting eyes,
The best charm under the sun,
The charm of God, the All-great,
Charm of Mary, charm of God,
Charm of Michael the strenuous,
Who bestowed on the sun its strength.

Such spells and charms, however, were by no means the only form of treatment available to the Highlanders. Even the ordinary clansfolk had a considerable knowledge of herbs and plants that could be used as medicines, and there were always a few men and women in each glen who were skilled in mixing the various herbs into compounds that would cure their sick neighbours. Among their prescriptions were foxglove for dropsy and heart disease, and mint for flatulence; and we now know that these plants do indeed help people suffering from those complaints.

Most of the ordinary clansfolk would depend on the local herbalist for treatment, but the chiefs and richer cadets might have more skilled medical assistance. From the fourteenth century onwards certain Highland families began to specialise in medicine. They became highly skilled doctors, and some of them went to Scottish, English and continental universities to study.

THE CLAN COMMUNITY   If all the various treatments failed to cure a clansman and he became a permanent invalid, then his family and indeed the whole clan would help to provide for him. Since all the clansmen believed that they were kinsfolk descended from the same ancestors, they were therefore ready to help each other in time of need. All this gave the clansmen a tremendous feeling of security, for they knew that they belonged to a community that cared for each and every one of them.

FOSTERAGE   One of the clan customs which helped to make the clansmen feel that they were members of a real family was fosterage, the practice whereby the chiefs had their sons brought up by foster-parents. The foster-father was often an ordinary clansman who had given exceptional service to the clan, and the boys lived with him as if he were their own father. In this way the people came to know the future chief intimately, and he became familiar with the lives of the ordinary clansmen.

The close ties thus forged between the chiefs and their followers encouraged the ordinary clansmen to feel that the triumphs and achievements of the chief and the clan were their very own. Even the poorest and weakest man could claim that he was a member of a community which had a glorious history and tradition. It was this feeling that led one clansman of the Clan MacLean to declare proudly: "I am poor but well born; thank God I am a MacLean."

5 · *A Foe to be Feared*

THE distinctive way of life, customs and language of the clansmen helped to set them apart from the people living in the Lowlands of Scotland. They were also cut off by the great Highland mountain ranges and by the lack of good roads. It is not surprising that for long periods of time the clansmen were much more concerned with their own affairs and with their feuds and quarrels than with what was happening in Edinburgh and elsewhere in Scotland.

In the seventeenth century, however, the clansmen began to play a much more important role in the affairs of Scotland and even of England. During the 1640s there was a Civil War in Scotland, as there was in England. Most of the people in the Lowlands had risen up against the policies of King Charles I, but the majority of the Highland clans remained loyal. In 1644 the Marquis of Montrose raised a royal army in the Highlands, and soon the clansmen were winning great victories over the King's enemies. Montrose was a brilliant military leader, and within a year he and his Highlanders had gained control of Scotland for King Charles. In 1645 he set out to take his army to England to support the King there, but at Philiphaugh near the Border he was surprised and defeated by an enemy army.

THE HIGHLAND CHARGE   The victories won by the Highland army under Montrose shocked and astounded the Lowlanders. They had been quite confident that their own forces, armed as they were with artillery, muskets and bayonets, were much more than a match for the clansmen with their claymores and shields. But it soon became clear that the tactics the clansmen adopted of charging furiously and wildly against their enemies gave them a decided advantage. Muskets and cannons took a considerable time to load, and only a few rounds could be fired before the waves of clansmen were upon the Lowland lines. And at close quarters the old-fashioned weapons of the Highlanders were terribly effective. The Lowland infantryman would lunge forward with his musket and bayonet, but the clansman easily parried this with his shield. Then in one mighty swing he brought his claymore down on the unprotected head of the unfortunate enemy soldier.

In the years after 1644, many Lowland and English armies were called upon to face the clansmen in battle, and thousands of men came to know and fear the Highland charge. Before they advanced, the clansmen would throw off their plaids. As they charged, they screamed their Gaelic war-cries and brandished their claymores, and the sight of these terrible warriors rushing towards them struck terror into the hearts of their foes. Often the enemies of the clansmen were so panic-stricken that their lines would break and scatter after they had fired only one wild shot.

Yet if a Highland charge was a terrifying weapon that could win battles, the clansmen had certain weaknesses as soldiers. They lacked discipline, and only a brilliant leader like Montrose could form them into a real army. The clansmen also disliked long campaigns, especially if they were called upon to leave the Highlands. Often after a victory large numbers of men would depart to take the loot they had captured to their homes. These failings helped to cause the defeat of Montrose at Philiphaugh, for the majority of the Highlanders had left his army when he decided to march to England.

The Highland charge

THE JACOBITES   There were several other occasions in the seventeenth and eighteenth centuries when the Highlanders played an important part in national affairs. Many of the clansmen remained loyal to the Stewart royal family after King James had to flee into exile in 1688 and William of Orange became King of England and of Scotland. They believed that James was still the rightful king, and they were given the name of "Jacobites", from the Latin word "Jacobus" meaning James. Later, after the Union of England and Scotland in 1707, and after the Hanoverians came to the throne in 1714, the Jacobite clans took part in a rebellion in

1715. They aimed to put the son of James on the throne of England and Scotland, but the rebellion was badly led, and ended in failure.

THE '45   Several years later there was another Jacobite rebellion. In July 1745, Prince Charles, the grandson of King James, landed at Moidart on the west coast of Scotland with six companions. The clan chiefs were utterly dismayed, for they had been hoping that he would bring French troops with him. Cameron

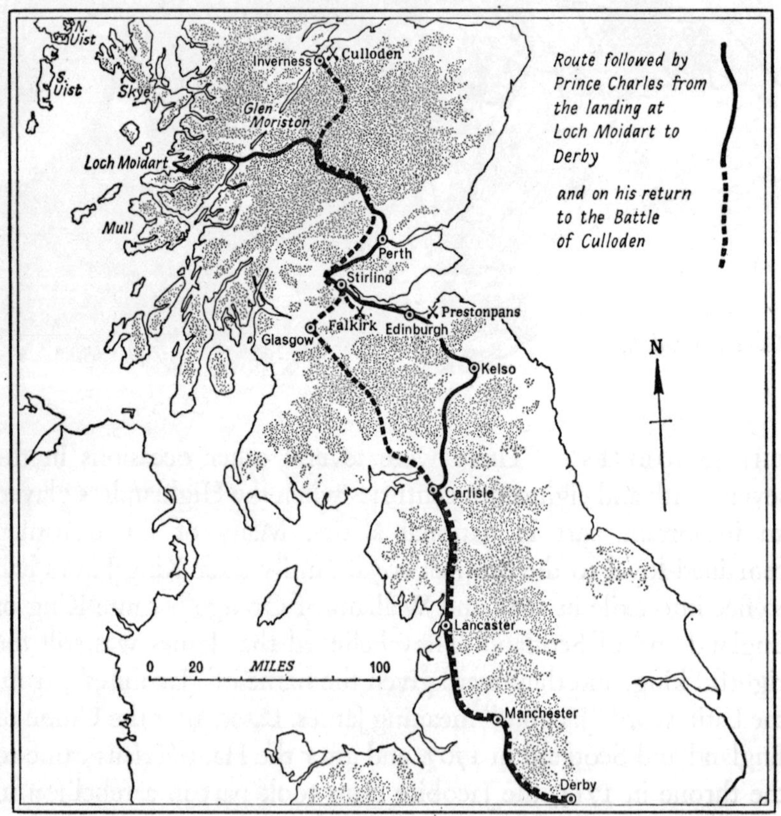

Routes of the '45 Rebellion

of Lochiel, the chief of Clan Cameron, tried to persuade the Prince to return to France, but Prince Charles refused to leave Scotland, declaring proudly: "I will erect the Royal Standard and proclaim that Charles Stewart has come over to claim the crown of his ancestors. And Lochiel may stay at home, and from the newspapers learn the fate of his Prince!"

At once Lochiel was won over by the charm and courage of the young prince, and he vowed to follow him whatever the cost. His example brought other chiefs and clans to support Charles, and soon he had a considerable army under his command.

Marching south from the Highlands, Prince Charles occupied Edinburgh and then defeated a Government army at Prestonpans. After a short delay, he led his army across the Border into England, and by December, 1745, he had reached Derby. There was a panic in London, but now the Prince's advisers urged him to turn back. Reluctantly he agreed, and wearily the Highland army trudged back across the Border into Scotland. The Jacobites won a last victory at Falkirk, but finally in April 1746 they were defeated at Culloden Moor near Inverness by an army under the command of the Duke of Cumberland.

The clansmen were badly led at Culloden. The Prince waited too long before giving the order to charge, and thus his army suffered terrible casualties as its ranks were pounded with grape-shot by the Government artillery. When at last the clansmen did charge and reached the Government lines, they discovered that their enemies had been trained in new tactics by the Duke of Cumberland. Each man in the front rank lunged forward with his bayonet, not at the clansman coming immediately towards him, but at the man to his right. This Highlander would have his arm raised to strike with his claymore, and so he would have no defence against the bayonet thrust. In this way the Government soldiers were able to equal the Highlanders in close-quarter fighting, and they successfully threw back the Highland charge.

So despite all the bravery and courage of the clansmen, the '45 Rebellion was finally crushed. Nevertheless their achievements were truly astonishing. The Jacobite army never numbered more than 8,000 men, for several clans refused to join the rising, and some (like the Campbells) fought on the Government side. If the clans had been united and the 20,000 men that they could raise had all supported the Prince, then surely he would have swept his enemies aside and become the ruler of Great Britain.

THE ESCAPE OF THE PRINCE   After the defeat of the Jacobites at Culloden, Prince Charles was forced to flee and hide in the hills. Government troops swarmed over the whole of the High-lands and Islands looking for him, and many Highland men and women risked their lives to help him, for it meant certain death to shelter him. A £30,000 reward was offered for any information leading to his capture, but no clansman came forward to claim this huge sum of money.

FLORA MACDONALD   Among the many Highlanders who came to the assistance of the Prince in his desperate situation was a young lady of twenty-four named Flora MacDonald. She was visiting friends in South Uist when Prince Charles was brought to the house where she was staying. There were many soldiers in the neighbourhood, and it was essential that he should get away from the island. Bravely she offered to help. The Prince was dressed as a woman and acted as her maid. Boldly they set out past the soldiers, and then when they were clear of them they sailed in a small boat to Skye. By her courage, Flora MacDonald played an important part in helping the Prince to escape from his enemies and at length reach France.

RODERICK MACKENZIE   Another Highlander who played a vital part in the escape of Prince Charles was an officer in the Jacobite army named Roderick MacKenzie. He had fought right through the campaign and after Culloden he went into hiding in Glen Moriston, not far from Loch Ness. While he was there, he learnt that the Prince was in the neighbourhood and that troops were closing in on him.

Often men had declared that Roderick MacKenzie looked surprisingly like the Prince, and now he decided to make use of this resemblance. Purposefully he allowed himself to be seen by a party of soldiers. The troops thought he was the Prince, and after a desperate pursuit they managed to corner him. He defended himself bravely, but the soldiers poured musket fire into his body and he fell mortally wounded. With his last breath he exclaimed: "Alas, you have slain your Prince!"

Now quite certain that they had indeed killed Prince Charles, the soldiers carried the head to Fort Augustus to claim the reward. The hunt for the Prince was slackened, and by the time it was discovered that the dead man was only a clansman, Prince Charles had escaped from the area. Later a memorial cairn was erected to Roderick MacKenzie on the spot where he died, and it still stands as a witness to his tremendous courage and self-sacrifice.

HIGHLAND REGIMENTS   The defeat of the Jacobite forces at Culloden effectively destroyed the fighting power of the clans (see p. 50), but the military exploits of the clansmen were by no means ended. After a few years the Government decided to raise Highland regiments to form part of the British Army. Several chiefs and leading Highlanders were given commissions to raise these regiments from among the clansmen.

The newly formed Highland regiments were first in action during the Seven Years' War (1756–63). They quickly won a fine military reputation, and soon many tales were being told of the courage of the Highland soldiers. One story described the bravery of a party of Highlanders who were taken prisoner by North American Indians. Twelve men endured savage torture without flinching, but the next man screamed for mercy. He told the Indians of a magic ointment which protected men from sword and spear, and promised to give them the formula if they would free him. Fascinated, they allowed him to concoct a herbal mixture which he smeared on his neck. Then he indicated that the strongest Indian should try to strike off his head with a sword. As the Highlander's head fell, the Indians gasped and realised that he had escaped torture by tricking them; but his sheer, cold courage won their admiration, and they let the rest of his comrades go.

The good work done by the Highland regiments in the Seven Years' War encouraged the Government to raise further units during the American War of Independence (1775–83) and during the French Revolutionary and Napoleonic Wars (1793–1815). In battle after battle in these and later wars they proved their fighting qualities, and steadily the fame of the Highland soldiers increased. Soon such regiments as the Argyll and Sutherland Highlanders, the Seaforths, the Cameron Highlanders, the Gordon Highlanders, the Highland Light Infantry were regarded as being among the finest in the British Army. During the First and Second World Wars, some of the Highland regiments were formed into the 51st Highland Division, and this division became noted for its fury in attack. The Germans in the First World War came to dread the sight of the Highlanders charging towards them in their kilts, and called them "the Ladies from Hell"!

CONCLUSION   We have seen that the Highlanders have played an important part in Scottish and British affairs throughout the centuries. On several occasions they came close to altering the whole course of British history, and they were for long a power to be feared by any government which they opposed. Even after the defeat at Culloden, they played a vital role in our history. Their war-like spirit was enlisted in the Highland regiments, and Highland soldiers proudly carried the arms of Great Britain to victory in every part of the world. No government ever received better service from any body of men, and the history of the British Empire is closely entwined with the story of the clansmen in their military regiments.

HIGHLAND REGIMENTS TODAY
a. 1st Reconnaissance Squadron (N.Z. Scottish), Royal New Zealand Armoured Corps   b. The Transvaal Scottish   c. The Royal Highland Regiment (The Black Watch)   d. The Royal New Brunswick Regiment

6 · *Exiles from the Glens*

WHILE the Highland soldiers were winning fame and glory in the wars fought by Britain after 1745, the whole way of life in the Highland glens was being completely transformed. The British Government had been so alarmed by the '45 Rebellion that it was determined to overthrow the society that had made such rebellions possible. Brutally and ruthlessly it set about destroying the clan system.

In the first place those Highlanders who had taken part in the Rebellion were treated with terrible severity. Wounded clansmen found lying helpless on Culloden Moor were stabbed to death with bayonets or shot. Of those taken prisoner, every tenth man was executed. The remainder were herded into filthy and stinking prisons and many died of gaol fever. Those who survived were transported to the American colonies and sold as servants and labourers. Thus only a very few of the men who had left the glens to fight for Prince Charles were ever able to return to their homes.

Against the families and kinsfolk of the rebel clansmen the Government acted with equal cruelty. The Duke of Cumberland led his army into the heart of the Highlands to punish the clans who had fought in the Rebellion. Fugitives were shot, homes and clachans were burnt down, and the cattle and herds were driven off. Throughout the winter of 1746–7 large numbers of women and children were forced to sleep on the hillsides, and many died of hunger and exposure.

Yet even this was not enough for the British Government. In 1747 an Act was passed through Parliament, taking away the legal powers of the clan chiefs. Other Acts were passed forbidding the Highlanders to carry arms, to wear Highland dress, or to play the bagpipes. The Government also showed itself hostile to the Gaelic language, and efforts were made to stamp it out.

These actions achieved their aim in destroying much of the old Highland way of life and in weakening the ties between the chiefs and their clansfolk. Some chiefs did continue to regard themselves as the "fathers" of their people, but many became more interested in making as much money as possible from their estates. They therefore began to evict clansmen from their clachans and to turn their glens into sheep farms. Later in the nineteenth century, when rich men from the south wished to obtain lands for sport and shooting, the sheep were replaced by deer.

Some of the clansmen who were driven from their homes were given land near the coast. There they lived as crofters, cultivating their small patches of rocky soil and fishing in the sea. They

lived mainly on potatoes and herrings, but frequently they suffered serious hardships and famines. In the 1840s the Highlands experienced a grim potato famine like that in Ireland, and there was mass suffering and starvation.

THE MIGRANTS   As the old way of life in the Highlands collapsed, many clansmen decided to leave their homeland. Some went south to the towns and cities of the Lowlands, and some crossed the Border into England. Many of the Highlanders prospered in their new homes, and some of them became rich and famous.

THE EMIGRANTS   Other clansmen went further afield. Even before the '45 Rebellion some Highlanders had sailed for the British colonies, but after Culloden far more people decided to emigrate. Some went to Canada, the United States or the West Indies, and later large numbers sailed for Australia, New Zealand and South Africa.

Often the exiles would meet together in ceilidhs to sing all the old familiar Gaelic songs, and their longing for the homeland is beautifully expressed in this famous song written in 1829:

> From the lone shieling of the misty island
> Mountains divide us, and the waste of seas—
> Yet still the blood is strong, the heart is Highland,
> And we in dreams behold the Hebrides.

Despite their regrets at leaving the Highlands of Scotland, the Highland emigrants and their children very quickly became loyal citizens of their adopted lands. Many Highlanders and their descendants rose to the highest positions in their new countries, and they played an important part in their affairs. The first Prime Minister of the Confederation of Canada in 1867, for instance, was John Alexander MacDonald, the son of a Highlander evicted from his croft in Sutherland. Sir Robert Menzies, one of the most famous politicians and Prime Ministers in modern Australia, has a Highland name and is descended from emigrants who came from Perthshire in Scotland. The Prime Minister of New Zealand from 1940 to 1949, Mr. Peter Fraser, was himself a Highlander born in Easter Ross.

In the United States, too, many Highlanders and the descendants of Highlanders became prominent in politics, trade and industry. One Highlander from Argyll, a certain Lachlan Mac-Gillvray, even played an important part in Indian affairs. In the eighteenth century he settled in Georgia and married an Indian woman. He had a son Alexander who later became a chieftain of the Creek Indians and caused the United States Government a great deal of trouble.

LEGACY OF THE CLANSMEN   With the departure of so many men and women, the Highlands were left with a sadly reduced population, and great stretches of countryside were given over to sheep and deer. Large numbers of Highlanders, however, did remain, and today their descendants continue to live on their ancestral lands where they still preserve many of the old ways. Gaelic is still spoken by many thousands of people, and ceilidhs and stories of the bygone days are very, very popular. But the clan system has disappeared, and the people living in the Highlands have become in effect ordinary citizens of Great Britain.

Yet though the clan system has disappeared, and though many Highlanders have left the glens, the clansmen did in a strange way

Balmoral Castle

win a real triumph. For centuries the Lowlanders and the English had feared and scorned them, but within fifty years of Culloden they were coming to think of everything Highland as romantic and fascinating. During the nineteenth century, Lowland tailors began to design all sorts of strange new tartans; for, whereas the English had once thought that kilts and tartans were barbaric, now these became extremely fashionable. Soon everyone was claiming that they had some Highland connection that entitled them to wear a particular tartan. Even the British Royal Family, which had once been the enemy of the Jacobite clans, came to take a real interest in the Highlands and in Highland traditions. Queen Victoria began spending her holidays at Balmoral Castle on Deeside, and her husband, Prince Albert, devised a new tartan for the Royal Family to wear!

As the movement glorifying everything Highland grew stronger, clan societies were founded in Lowland and English cities, and in many countries throughout the world. Today there are innumerable branches of the Clan Donald Society, the Clan

Campbell Society and many others. Some clan societies hold gatherings in Scotland, and often visitors from overseas countries attend them. Pipe bands were also formed in many places, and in Scotland Highland Games with such traditional events as tossing the caber and Highland dancing became increasingly popular.

So the spirit and traditions of the clansmen linger on in the minds and hearts of countless numbers of people today, though the old clans have vanished. Highland courage, heroism, loyalty, dress and whole way of life has a great appeal to us now. Across the centuries we can recognise that the clansmen of the Scottish Highlands were indeed a remarkable and a great people; and those who can claim to be descended from them have every reason to be proud of their ancestors.

Time Chart

Date	THE CLANSMEN	EVENTS IN BRITISH HISTORY
1200		
	Forming of the clans	
1300		
	Lord of the Isles	
	'Wolf of Badenoch'	
1400		
	James I seizes chiefs at Inverness	James I of Scotland
	Title of Lord of the Isles forfeited	James IV of Scotland
1500		
	Lachlan MacLean and the Campbells	
		Reformation in Scotland
1600		
	MacGregors outlawed Decline of the MacDonalds' power	Union of the Crown
	'Another for Hector'	Civil War in England and Scotland Montrose: Battle of Philiphaugh Cromwell: Battle of Inverkeithing
	Massacre of Glencoe	The Glorious Revolution
1700	Execution of Macpherson Rob Roy MacGregor	Union of the Parliaments The 1715 Rebellion
	Emigration Redcoats in the Highlands (Flora MacDonald Highland dress forbidden and Roderick MacKenzie)	The '45 Rebellion Bonnie Prince Charlie: Battle of Culloden
	Highland Regiments formed	The Seven Years' War
		The American War of Independence
		French Revolutionary and
1800		Napoleonic Wars
	Highlanders evicted by landlords	
		Queen Victoria crowned
	Balmoral Castle built	
	Sir John A. MacDonald Prime Minister of Canada	Federation of Canada
1900		

Books to Read

Grant, I. F. *Highland Folk Ways* (Routledge and Kegan Paul)
Grant, I. F. *Everyday Life on an Old Highland Farm* (Longmans)
Kermack, W. R. *The Scottish Highlands: A Short History* (Johnson and Bacon)
Leodhas, Sorche Nic *Gaelic Ghosts* (The Bodley Head)
(Clara MacLeod)
Linklater, E. *The Prince in the Heather* (Hodder and Stoughton)
Moncreiffe, Sir Iain *The Highland Clans* (Barrie and Rockliff)
Prebble, J. *Culloden* (Penguin Books)
Ed. Robb, Dewar M. *Poems and Ballads of Scottish History* (Blackie)

Novels and Stories

Broster, D. K. *The Flight of the Heron* (Heinemann)
Broster, D. K. *The Gleam in the North* (Heinemann)
Broster, D. K. *The Dark Mile* (Heinemann)
Drever, H. *Tales of the Scottish Clans* (The Moray Press)
Fidler, K. *Lanterns over the Lune* (Lutterworth)
Fidler, K. *The White Cockade Passes* (Lutterworth)
Fidler, K. *The Droving Lad* (Lutterworth)
Lane, J. *The Champion of the King* (Evans)
Mitchison, N. *The Bull Calves* (Cape)

Index